I0478699

Want Priority Access to FREE eBooks Additional Materials for this Book?

As we release NEW eBooks, we offer them for FREE for a limited time. You will be the FIRST one to know when they are FREE. Join 1000's of insiders who are getting access to FREE Kindle book promotions weekly.

Click HERE for FREE additional material and FREE eBooks- www.rictamilypublishing.com

Chapter I: What is Financial Freedom?

There are many ways to express Financial Independence. Hence, it is not easy to achieve it.

Financial Freedom defined

Financial freedom is also known as financial independence. It is the state describing the sufficiency of personal wealth to sustain the cost of living, without having to actively work for basic commodities. The income is greater than the expenses for financially independent people.

Assets: anything a person possesses that can be liquidated when he or she incurs debt. On the other hand, liability is the responsibility of a person to provide compensation for debt incurred.

Age and income are not the basis of financial independence. Anyone can be considered financially independent, regardless of how old or young or how much he or she earns for a living. However, the capacity to generate money enough to suffice their need, aside from their primary occupation, is what matters in the aspect of financial independence.

Different views on Financial Freedom

This is a powerful concept. Often, the majority receives this as a good thing. We want to achieve it and admire those who already have. Most people who are in their 20s have this mission and tag-line that states "Get a head start on freedom".

However, some people might relate financial independence to retirement, never having to work again, being free from debt, doing what they want for a living and not relying on others for money.

The tricky part is, if you are concerned about your income, are you financially independent?

Problem with the definitions

There is no specific correct definition. The only basis is the sufficiency of the asset over expenses. However, in the definitions provided above, lies a common ground, which is being qualitative.

The qualitative aspects of the definition shall play as motivation to set goals and achieve them. But, if you are not aware of the endpoint, what will be your basis of setting up the goals?

Chapter II: Being Practical or Being Technical?

Since the topic of financial independence is broad, the approaches for the achievement of financial independence are also broad. Let us take a look at the practical and technical practices in achieving financial independence.

Practicality defined

The word practical can mean many things. These are:

- Relating to reality
- Appropriate or suitable for use in actual situation
- Reasonable to do or use
- Likely to succeed
- Manifests in practice or action
- Being in effect or actively engaged in course of action
- Capable of being put to use
- Qualified for practical training or practice

Hence, practicality is the application of the things listed above.

Technicality defined

Technicality covers a wide scope. Hence it includes:

- Relating to practical use of science or machines
- Teaching skills rather than ideas
- Special knowledge on how a machine works or how particular work is done

- Relating to technique

Practicality vs. Technicality

Practicality may pertain to the management of what you already have. For example, you have a fixed income of $100. To obtain financial independence, that is to have your income higher than your expenses, you must do something to control expenses. This includes budgeting, cost-cutting, setting your priorities or taking excessive leisure's out of your life.

On the other hand, technicality covers the procedure to attain or achieve something. For example, you have affixed income of $100. In order to obtain financial independence, you will resort to activities which you think will increase your income. These activities may take the forms of investments, management of borrowings, applying for insurances and doing other jobs aside from your primary source of living.

Chapter III: Attitudes Required to Achieve Financial Freedom

Financial freedom is not a matter of how much your wealth is, or how much money is waiting for you when you finally decided to retire. It is more about the self- fulfilling feeling of being satisfied with how your money works for you and your necessities. Here are the key attitudes needed to achieve financial freedom.

Commitment

Being committed means having you involved in or dedicating yourself to a specific matter. This is to be taken together with the obligation. This force drives you to set goals on how to achieve a desired result. If you are not committed to what you are doing, the foundation of your desire for the achievement of the goal is weak.

The same is true with the commitment to achieve financial freedom. This is not just about telling yourself that you want to be financially independent. It is more about driving yourself to take action to achieve your desired results. This is also a long-term contract.

Self- discipline

If you have already decided to commit yourself to attain financial freedom, it does not end there. It is a mere drive; hence, it should be accompanied with action. This action is what we call self-discipline. This term is associated with self- control.

Self- control is the capacity to control behavior, desires or emotion to perform a function, particularly relating to self or society. Psychologically speaking, this also pertains to self-regulation. This is an essential step in achieving goals and avoiding impulses or emotions that may hinder the achievement of goals.

Necessity over luxury

This attitude is important in achieving financial freedom. More often than not, we are preoccupied with our wants which have already exceeded our needs. We tend to spend or crave luxurious items when, in reality, they have cheap equivalents with the same purpose or quality.

In order to effectively manage your money, you should know what to do or buy and what to not do or not buy. This will help you choose better alternatives.

Effective management of resources

This attitude will help you with the effective utilization of your given resources. It takes planning to determine whether your money will be productive if invested in certain activities. It also takes careful weighing of opportunities and cost before allowing your money to leave your hands.

In many cases, people with sufficient resources tend to fail in becoming financially independent. This is because of the confidence regarding sufficiency. People with limited resources tend to succeed in becoming financially independent because of the challenge of lacking sufficiency.

Chapter IV: Budgeting and Cost Cutting

In this chapter, some of the practical ways of achieving financial freedom will be discussed. This chapter will focus on budgeting and cost- cutting.

Budgeting

It is a plan to be used as a guideline for saving and spending purposes. The key factor in budgeting is to know where your money is allotted and to spend less than what you earn. An effective budget plan can ensure that you pay bills on time, achieve financial goals and make room for contingencies.

Principles of Budgeting

Conservatism

In budgeting, you must understand the actual results, in some cases, may vary from the planned results. Since budgeting is a forecast, it does not render absolute assurance. In doing a budget, you must put a margin, which is more effective if you underestimate your income and overestimate your expenses. Therefore, you can make room for possible contingencies.

Preparation time

Budgeting cannot and should not be done within a few hours. An ample time is necessary to weigh what to include and what to omit, so that an efficient and effective budget plan will be produced. Also, the budget plan must be flexible and include the possibility of new information affecting it. Consultations and research are essential parts of budgeting.

Cost- cutting

These are measures implemented to decrease expenses:

Writing down your daily expenses

Keeping track of your expenses is not a hard job. All you need is a handy notebook to list all of your expenses daily. You must also list the costs to be paid on a monthly basis, such as utilities and rent. From you record, you can now easily identify the costs to be cut off or regulated.

Cut down utilities

In order to lessen your expenses, you must know how to save, not only money, but resources. If you are spending a lot on water, electricity and phone bills, minimize their usage. You can do simple things such as turning off the faucet while brushing your teeth; turning off the lights when not in use; avoid phone chatting when not necessary; and recycle water when watering plants or washing your car.

Chapter V: Priorities

In order to stay on the path to achieve something, you must know your priorities. Priorities play a significant and vital role in achieving financial freedom.

Priorities

Priorities are items we first dealt with in the belief that they are more important than others. They are the things we care for the most compared to other things. In setting priorities, we must consider our desired results. This will provide the basis for identifying what's important and what's not.

Setting up your priorities

Think and reflect about things with real importance

There is a point in your life when you need to take a little break. This break will help you reflect on your current status. This will also help you to realize the things you have already done and the things you ought to do.

In achieving financial freedom, you need to know what matters to you the most. As mentioned earlier, financial freedom is best obtained when you are already satisfied with how your money works for you and your necessities.

Before buying something or doing something, you must ask yourself if these things or events are important. For example, if you have the vice of smoking or drinking, are they important and necessary? Here are some questions to ask:

1. Will I benefit if I buy or do this?
2. What will be the cost of doing or buying this?
3. Can I live without doing or buying this?

    4. Yes, occasional leisure is not bad. However, developing it as a habit will ruin your goals to achieve financial freedom. Remember the principle; anything taken in **excess of moderate is bad.**

Understanding Alternatives

    5. Are you after the brand or its quality? Take, for example, a visit to the grocery store for a carton of milk. There are several brands, namely A, the leading brand amounting to $20; brand B, the not-so-popular brand amounting to $15. Aware of the things you should consider, you have evaluated that both products contain the same nutritional ingredients and ratios. Should you buy the leading brand or settle for the cheaper brand with the same quality?

Chapter VI: Investments

Resources idled are resources wasted. If you happen to have excess money for your daily undertakings, what will you do?

Investment

In general, investments are items acquired with the belief that it will generate income or appreciate in the future. On the other hand, in economics, investment is the purchase of goods that is not to be consumed today, but will be used in the future to incur wealth. Another definition is in finance, where investments are monetary assets purchased with the idea that it will provide income or will be sold at a higher price in the future.

The most common ground for the meanings stated above is that, investments were believed to generate income. There are several types of investments that will help you achieve financial freedom.

Investment in Bonds

These are debt securities. Upon purchasing one, you are actually lending your money to a municipality, government, federal agency, and corporation or to an entity known as the issuer. In exchange for your lending of the money, the issuer issues you a bond, which contains the specified rate of interest and the principal amount to be paid when it matures or due.

Most investors prefer bonds because of its predictable income stream. Usually, bonds pay semiannual interest. They also invest in bonds to preserve capital investment.

Investment in Stock

As compared to bonds, stocks are shares of ownership instead of debt securities. Owning a stock means that you are a part owner or shareholder of a specific corporation. The stock market is where stocks are traded. Investors tend to allot money on stocks because of the benefit they can derive from the company's value after a specific period of time.

Because of owning a stock and being a shareholder, you are now part of the company. You can now take part on the success and growth of the company through its stock price appreciation and by earning and claiming your dividends.

Chapter VII: Advantages and Disadvantages of Borrowings

Borrowing money from others will make you solve your current debts and liabilities. However, due to its accumulation and the appurtenant interest, this can lead you to backslide and away from obtaining your financial freedom.

Borrowings

This is the act of receiving something in exchange for a value received, with the obligation to pay such thing with a greater value at a specified time in the future. This explains why borrowing large some of moneys from others will lead you to a harder way of recovering from financial distress.

Advantages of Borrowing

Immediate source of fund

When you are facing a crucial situation and you badly need for cash right away, the only feasible option is to borrow money from someone you know or from credit institutions. Even if you are knowledgeable enough that you will need to pay a greater compensation because of borrowing, you do not have other options to select.

Flexible terms of repayment

If you borrowed money from a family member, it is favorable because the repayment terms are flexible. It also lifts the burden of signing and filling up loan paperwork's.

Disadvantages of Borrowing

Paying back a higher amount

As you borrow money, the compensation is to pay a higher value. Given the fact that you have engaged in the crucial transaction because of the money borrowed, often, the interest attached to the borrowing is so high to compensate the benefit derived from the crucial transaction.

Accruing interest

You borrowed money to finance a certain transaction. This leads to the conclusion that you are in a financial distress. However, borrowing money is not the solution. If you are not capable to produce the principal, how can you pay the interest attached, which have accrued for a considerable period of time?

Chapter VIII: Insurances

Aside from investments, one can ensure his financial freedom through acquiring or applying for insurances. This will help lessen the burden of facing certain circumstances and situations.

Insurances

These are contracts or policies that an individual buys to obtain financial protection or reimbursements against specific losses.

Why buy insurance?

The need for buying life insurance is a hard decision to make. It can even be harder if you are still in a younger age. However, insurance helps you to ensure financial protection against losses.

The most common and obvious reason why a person buys a life insurance is because it can replace your income if you die prior to your dependents.

The term life insurance policy gives you an option of the insurance coverage ranging from 10 to 30 years.

Insurance as an investment

Most of the young professionals took insurance as an investment. For them, insurance can be a great addition to their investment portfolios. Investments have risks yet, undeniably, your cash can accrue greater value compared to its value when kept idle.

At the time when you will need cash to pay for your medical expenses, in case you become terminally ill, you may have the option to sell your policy to a vertical settlement company at a discounted price.

Chapter IX: Freelancing and other sources of Extra Income

You must not rely only on your primary source of income. You must also find jobs that will give you extra income without sacrificing your quality of work on your primary source; some of which are part- time jobs, freelancing and other sources of extra income.

Part- time jobs

Aside from working 8 hours a day in office or any other work, which gives rise to your primary income, you can also find part- time jobs which only requires about a portion of your time. In this manner, you have a sure and guaranteed earnings derived from your primary work and an additional income from your part- time job.

Your income from your primary job may cover living expenses and necessities. On the other hand, your income from part- time jobs may take part of your savings or allocation for contingencies.

Freelancing

Due to fast changing technology and globalization, there are many jobs offered as a freelance job. Freelance worker or freelancer refers to a person who is not necessarily committed to a

specific employer for a long- term setup. Also, it refers to someone who is self- employed. Often, freelancers are represented by an agency that resells their laborOne of the most popular freelancing jobs nowadays is the freelance writing. Because of the growing demand of contents for online sites and other media, there is a high demand for freelance writing. Your hard work and determination will be the basis of your earnings.

Business venture

Aside from working, you can also join business ventures or create one. The advantage is that you have the full control on how the business works. Your profit or loss is based on how you plan and strategize. Also, business ventures are one of the most successful ways to become rich.

Chapter X: Spending is Easy, Saving is Difficult

They say, things that are easy to do are the worse or inappropriate ones while those things which are difficult to do are those things which are right. Therefore, do the things that are difficult yet right. The same is true with investing and saving.

Spending

This is the act of using money to pay for something. It is also the act of allowing time to pass in a particular place or when performing a specific activity. It is also the usage of energy and effort in doing something. In short, it is the resources that we consume in exchange for something.

Based on human nature, we are natural givers. That is why, it is so easy for us to spend money, time, energy and effort to satisfy the transactions deemed necessary in our perspective. However, have we ever wondered if how many of these transactions are actually necessary?

To achieve financial freedom, we must refrain from spending too much on things that are not essential. This will pave way to a higher income compared to expenses. It was never easy to stop spending, but for the sake of achieving your goals, control it now.

Saving

This refers to the portion of something not spent or used. It is also the amount of money that has been put in a bank or similar location for future use over a specific time or period. However, taking a portion out of your income for saving purposes was never easy.

There are times that we tell ourselves that we will save. Say for instance, we will save 10% of our income. Yet, whether we put them on a bank or other location, we tend to use them for other purposes such as emergencies, or worst, vices. Because of this tendency, we find it hard to keep them.

To be able to achieve financial freedom, we must learn to save.

Savings help us ensure our future after retirement. It ensures us that we have something to consume when the time comes that we cannot work for our necessities.

Review Link

If you enjoyed this book, we would really appreciate it if you could leave us a positive REVIEW?

P.S. **You can** <u>CLICK HERE</u> **to go directly to the book page** and leave your review and/or purchase our other books above. Alternately, you can copy and paste this address into your browser --- http://amzn.to/1wCj3OE

Our Other Books

Anti-Cancer Diet: The Ultimate Guide in Fighting Cancer, Lowering Cancer Risk and Achieving Optimum Health

Gout Cure: Your Ultimate and Comprehensive Guide in Treating Gout Permanently

Anger, Stress and Fear: Your Personal Guide in Controlling Anger, Managing Stress and Overcoming Fear

Pilates for Beginners: The Essential Guide to Total Body Fitness, Strong Muscles and Lean Body

Stop Self-Sabotaging and Shift your Paradigm to Success: Your Ultimate Guide in Start Living the Life You Always Wanted

Chakras for Beginners: The Ultimate Guide to Balancing Chakras, Radiating Positive Energies and Strengthening Auras

CLICK HERE to go directly to our other books

The Ultimate Guide to Financial Freedom: Achieve Wealth, Attain Success and Manage Your Debt like the Rich

The True Nature of Intelligence: Musing on the Sumerian Culture from a Christian Perspective

The Ad: A Mail-Order Bride Romance Series

Gilgamesh - King in Quest for Immortality: An Extra-Biblical Proof for the Genesis Flood

Liver Cleanse and Detox Diet: The Ultimate Guide in Cleansing the Body, Eliminating Toxins and Losing Weight!

Top Ten Pets for Children: Tips on Care and Proper Choice for Your Child

Teeth Healing Through Oil Pulling: The Complete Guide in Natural Oral Care through the Benefits of Oil Pulling

Herbal Soap Making: How to Make Homemade Soaps that clean and Nurture the Body

10 Things You Need to Know About Ebola: Facts about the Virus, Symptoms, Quarantine and Prevention

CLICK HERE to go directly to our other books

Dedication

To our three blessings that have made RicTamily complete and continue to grow together in His loving embrace.

CLICK HERE to go directly to our author page

Disclaimer

The information in this book is in no way intended as medical advice. This book is not meant to be used, nor should it be used, to diagnose or treat any medical condition. The author disclaims responsibility for any adverse health effects that come in combination with the use of methods and suggestions presented in the book. The publisher and author are not responsible for any health or allergy needs that may require medical supervision and are not liable for any damages or negative consequences from any treatment, action, application or preparation, to any person reading or following the information in this book.

Copyright

All Rights Reserved. No part of this publication may be reproduced or transmitted in any form whatsoever, electronic, or mechanical, including photocopying, recording, or by any informational storage or retrieval system without express written, dated and signed permission from the author.

Contact: www.rictamilypublishing.com

THE END

www.ingramcontent.com/pod-product-compliance
Lightning Source LLC
Chambersburg PA
CBHW041617180526
45159CB00002BC/896